Cut some plastic [sha]pes, stamp, color the [des]igns, shrink… the [res]ults are a one-of-a-[kin]d charm bracelet that [is f]un to wear.

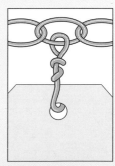

Easy & Fun Shrink[...]

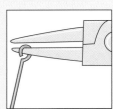

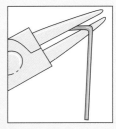

[B]asic Instructions

Sand plastic with 320 to [?] grit sandpaper in a cross-[hat]ch pattern.

[S]tamp design with heat-set [?] and color background [wit]h chalk or colored pencils.

Cut out design and punch [ho]les before shrinking.

[?] Place on medium weight [ca]rdboard or a teflon sheet. [Ba]ke in a regular or toaster [ov]en at 300° to 350°F for [ap]proximately 3 minutes. Or [he]at with a heat gun.

Charm Bracelet

MATERIALS: Clear and White shrink plastic sanded on one side • *Stamp Studio* rubber stamps (Americana tagit, rooster tagit, fruitful tagit, dress, Oriental doll, pear, vintage letter) • Black heat-set ink • Assorted colors of pigment ink • Chalk • Red and Black gel pens • Gold charm bracelet • Jump rings • 28 gauge Gold wire • Assorted metal and glass charms • 1/4" hole punch • 5/8" dowel • Needle-nose pliers • Heat gun • Spray matte sealer

INSTRUCTIONS: Stamp dress, pear and vintage letter on White shrink plastic. Color with chalk. Stamp Americana tagit and rooster tagit on White, color with pigment ink and dot rooster with gel pens. Stamp Clear shrink plastic with remaining stamps and color with pigment ink. Cut out shapes and punch holes in tops. Shrink plastic pieces. Shape Oriental doll over dowel while heating referring to instructions on page 25. Spray with sealer. Attach plastic shapes and charms to bracelet with jump rings or wire.

Shrink Art 101 Basic Tips

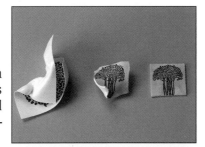

Certain things will happen when shrinking plastic. One is curling. Plastic will always curl as it shrinks. Expect it to happen, it is okay.

If plastic sticks to itself as it shrinks, allow to cool and then pull apart gently. You will hear a tiny 'snap' and the plastic will separate.

If the plastic looks like it will stick when heating with a heat gun, immediately take the heat off and pull apart. Continue to heat piece until flat. Plastic can be flattened gently with a piece of smooth cardboard.

How to Attach Charms with Wire

1. Bend wire at 90° with pliers.

2. Bend into partial loop. Slip over link in charm bracelet.

3. Close loop. Thread through charm, bend wire up and twist as shown.

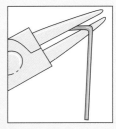

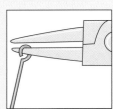

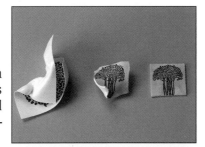

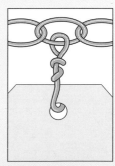

Designing with Shrink Plastic

Sanding prepares the surface to take colors and gives the finished piece a soft, velvety finish. Sand in crosshatch pattern until gloss is removed.

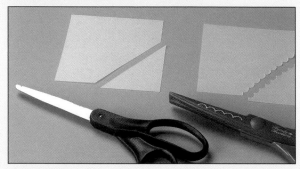

Cutting Plastic. Always cut plastic shapes in the same direction.

Colors will be softer on Translucent plastic than on White. The end project you are designing will dictate the color of plastic you use.

Inks. Heat-set inks are permanent after heating and maintain vibrant colors. If smearing is a problem, heat-set inks can be applied and then left to dry for a day. Inks will not be permanent but can be cut without smearing. Apply to the plastic directly from the pad or with sponges and stipple brushes.

Permanent inks dry very quickly and are permanent without heating. Use when you want to stamp, color and shrink. They adhere well to unsanded plastic.

Note: Do not use dye inks on sanded shrink plastic as they will bleed.

The Chalks will darken when the plastic is shrunk using an oven or a heat gun.

Stained Glass

It is easy to achieve a stained glass effect using shrink plastic. An image is stamped on one side of the shrink plastic and the color floats through to the glossy front. Use stained glass for jewelry or shapes on frames.

Open
Correct w
to open
jumprin

Rollagraph Earrings & Necklace

by Sue

MATERIALS: Clear shrink plastic sanded on one side • *Clearsnap* R graphs (Designer #33266, Designer #33271, Designer #33285 and Ze #235) • Black heat-set ink • Chalk • 24" Gold chain with clasp • Two pieces of Gold chain for earrings • Pair of Gold ear wires • 27 Gold 6 jump rings • ¼" hole punch • Decorative scissors • Needle-nose pliers

INSTRUCTIONS: Rub Red and Yellow, Blue and Green, Purple and E bands of chalk on sanded plastic. Using rollagraphs, apply patterns sanded side of plastic. Let dry overnight until ink has lost its luster. Us regular or decorative scissors, cut out irregular shapes. Allow for a li over 50% shrinkage. Punch holes ⅛" from one edge. Shrink shapes. Ap Gold ink to edges with a metallic pen. With jump rings, attach shapes every fifth link of necklace. Attach chain and add shapes to ear wires v jump rings

1. Rub bands of chalk on sanded Clear plastic.

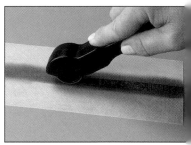

2. Apply patterns to sanded si of plastic with rollagraph.

3. Cut out design with plain and decorative scissors.

4. Cut shapes and punch ho ⅛" from top.

5. Shrink shapes.

6. Attach shapes to chain wi jump rings.

Little stained glass pieces glow with color on a lightweight necklace and earrings that will be beautiful additions to your jewelry collection.

Basic Information

1. There are two ways to work with stamps and plastic. One is to stamp and shrink and the other is to shrink and stamp. The look of the stamp will be very different.

2. Use stamps as design elements... as partial images or textures.

3. Use good craft scissors (or wavy scissors) to cut plastic to size.

4. Plastic pieces come out of the oven looking less than square.

Good shrink plastic will stay uniform to a certain degree but not precisely. Sometimes a rough look works and sometimes a smooth look. If a piece is not straight, trim with scissors and sand edges.

5. After sanding edges, color edge with a marker or run the edge through embossing ink and powder. Emboss.

6. To finish, spray with Clear sealer. Allow to dry.

Stamped Jewelry

Lovely jewelry designs have never been so easy to make. Just stamp and color shrink plastic, punch holes and shrink. Then combine the colorful pieces with beads to make necklaces, bracelets and earrings.

Blue & White Floral
Necklace & Bracelet

by Sue B

MATERIALS: Clear shrink plastic sanded on one side • *Clearsnap* Rollagraph
East Floral #644 • White heat-set ink • Blue chalk • 18" Silver chain with clasp
Silver barrel clasp for bracelet • 13 Pearl 5mm pony beads • 37 Silver 6mm ju
rings • ¼" hole punch • Decorative scissors • Needle-nose pliers

INSTRUCTIONS: Rub sanded side of plastic with Blue chalk. Using Rollagra
apply pattern to sanded side of plastic. Let dry overnight until ink has lost its l
ter. Cut out designs. Punch holes ⅛" from edge of leaves for necklace and ⅛
from ends of leaves for bracelet. Shrink plastic pieces.

For each necklace dangle, thread pony bead on one jump ring. Add a jump ri
on each side. Starting in center of chain, attach one jump ring to necklace cha
and other jump ring to necklace plastic piece. Add remaining pieces at 1" inte
vals.

For bracelet, thread 8 pony beads on jump rings. Attach one beaded jump ri
to one side of barrel clasp. Add jump ring and plastic piece. Continue adding
jump ring, beaded jump ring and jump ring between plastic pieces. End with jur
ring, beaded jump ring and other side of clasp.

Keepsakes Box

A plain papier-mâché box [be]comes a work of art with an [em]bossed finish and a shrink [pla]stic design raised on little feet.

[Pie]ce Box
by Steve Felton

[MA]TERIALS: 3½" square of Clear plastic sanded on [one] side • 1¾" x 2½" paper box •Geisha rubber [stam]p(eraser carved by Steve Felton) • Red and [Gol]d permanent ink • Black heat-set ink • Clear [emb]ossing powder • Colored pencils • Diamond [Glaz]e • Four 8mm and four 10mm wood balls • Heat [tool] • Paintbrush • Ultra Thin Bond adhesive

[INS]TRUCTIONS: Rub Red and Gold ink on box. While [wet], dip in Clear embossing powder, heat following [inst]ructions on page 15. Add 2 to 3 layers of ink and [pow]der to make all sides of box shiny. Shrink plastic [squ]are. Stamp Japanese lady on sanded back with [blac]k heat-set ink, let dry. Color with pencils. Brush [fron]t with Diamond Glaze, let dry. Glue 8mm balls on [cor]ners of plastic square and glue square on front of [box]. Glue 10mm balls on bottom of box for feet.

[Da]ngle Earrings
by Jane Roulston

[MA]TERIALS: Clear shrink plastic sanded on one side [• Cu]di-Kins deco flower background rubber stamp • [Per]manent inks • Colored pencils • 2 Gold ear wires [• 6] Gold head pins • E beads (Yellow, Pink, Green, [Tea]l) • 2 Green leaf beads • 2½" circle punch • ¼" [hol]e punch • Needle-nose pliers

[INS]TRUCTIONS: Cut 2 plastic 2½" circles. Punch [hol]es ⅛" from edge at top and bottom of circles. [Sta]mp images on glossy sides of plastic circles with [per]manent ink. Color images with colored pencils on [san]ded sides. Shrink and sand edges. Thread colored [bea]ds on head pins referring to photo. Make loops in [pin]s and attach to bottom holes. Attach ear wires to [top] holes.

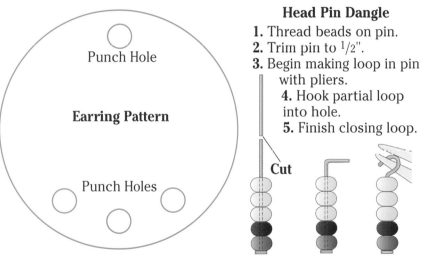

Punch Hole

Earring Pattern

Punch Holes

Head Pin Dangle
1. Thread beads on pin.
2. Trim pin to ½".
3. Begin making loop in pin with pliers.
   4. Hook partial loop into hole.
   5. Finish closing loop.

Cut

1. Sand one side of shrink plastic to remove gloss.

2. Cut two 2½" circles using a circle punch.

3. Stamp image on shiny plastic, let dry. Color on sanded side.

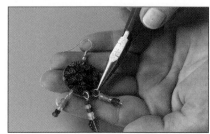

4. Shrink. Attach beaded head pins and ear wires.

Framed Pins

by Jane Rouls

This technique involves stamping before shrinking. Coloring c
be done before or after shrinking using chalks, colored pencils or
markers. Projects can be as simple as stamped images cut out an
colored or as elaborate as pins with framed miniatures.

MATERIALS: White shrink plastic sanded on one side • Assorted rubber stamp
Black heat-set ink • Assorted chalks, colored pencils or watercolors • 2³⁄₈", 3"
3³⁄₈" circle templates • 1" pin backs • Eye pins • Head pins • Assorted beads
charms • ¹⁄₄" hole punch • Needle-nose pliers • Sandpaper • Ultra Thin Bond
super glue

INSTRUCTIONS: Cut 3³⁄₈" circle with 2³⁄₈" opening for frame and 3" circle for ba
ground from sanded shrink plastic using patterns. Punch holes in frame opening
make cutting easier. Punch holes for beads or other embellishments. Stamp desi
images for gluing on pin background and cut out. Color frame and background w
chalks, colored pencils or watercolors. Shrink frame pieces in toaster oven. Cc
and shrink or shrink and color images for pin. Assemble frame with glue. Thr
beads and charms on head or eye pins and add to pin. Glue pin back in place.

Basic Information for Framed Pins

Cut a 3³⁄₈" diameter frame, 2³⁄₈" diameter opening and 3" diameter background pieces using patterns provided from White sanded shrink plastic.

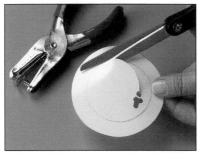

1. Transfer patterns to sanded shrink plastic, punch the holes and cut out.

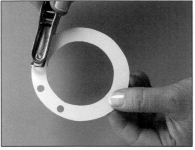

2. Punch holes for beaded accents using ¹⁄₄" hole punch.

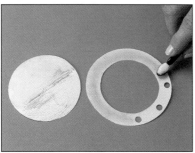

3. Color frame and background with chalks, colored pencils or watercolors. Shrink.

4. Color and shrink or shrink and color embellishments for pin.

5. Assemble pin with Ultra Thin Bond or super glue.

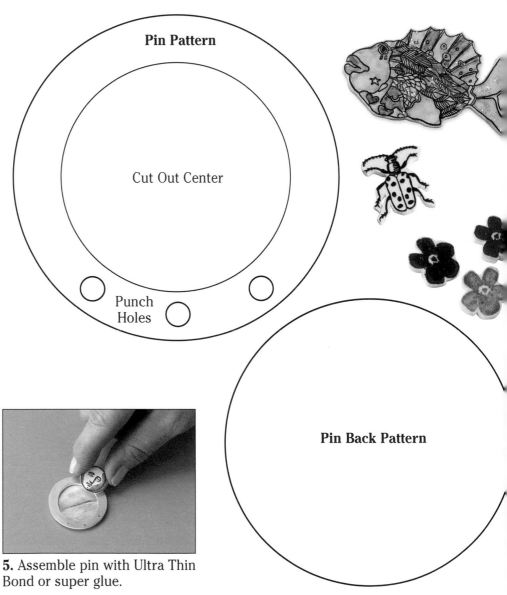

Pin Pattern

Cut Out Center

Punch Holes

Pin Back Pattern

You can make a pin to match any ~~od~~, event or even the print in a ~~orite~~ outfit. Just stamp and shrink ~~signs~~ and glue on a pin. Then add ~~ded~~ dangles for a finishing touch.

~~ncers~~ Pin

~~TERIALS:~~ *Viva Las Vegas* dancers rubber stamp • 3 ~~d~~ head pins • Beads (3 Pink E, 3 Clear E, 2 Blue E, 2 ~~k~~ 4mm faceted, 5mm Pink textured, 2 Blue 5mm ~~le)~~

~~sh~~ Pin

~~TERIALS:~~ *Paula Best* fish rubber stamp • 2 Gold ~~d~~ pins • Gold eye pin • Beads (3 Gold 4mm, 2 Pink ~~rt~~, Pink E, 2 Amethyst 6mm faceted, 2 Turquoise ~~n~~, Turquoise diamond) • Gold shell charm • Pink ~~er~~ glue

~~e~~ Pin

~~TERIALS:~~ Bee and flower rubber stamps • 2 Gold ~~d~~ pins • Gold eye pin • Beads (8 Turquoise E, 2 Red ~~3~~ Turquoise 6mm faceted, Red 6mm) • Gold leaf ~~rm~~

~~use~~ Pin

~~TERIALS:~~ *Claudia Rose* rubber stamps (ladybug, ~~ken~~, house, leaf, flower) • 2 Silver head pins • Sil-~~eye~~ pin • Beads (3 Turquoise E, 2 Yellow E, 3 Red E, ~~reen~~ 8mm disk, Yellow diamond) • Silver flower ~~rm~~

Head Pin Dangle

~~T~~hread beads on pin.
~~T~~rim pin to 1/2".
~~B~~end wire at 90° with ~~edle~~-nose pliers.
~~H~~ook partial loop ~~o~~ bottom hole.
~~F~~inish closing loop.

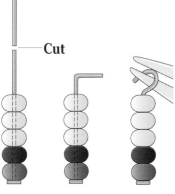

Eye Pin Dangle

~~O~~pen existing loop in ~~e~~ pin and add charm.
~~se~~ the loop.
~~T~~hread beads on pin ~~d~~ bend wire at 90° with ~~edle~~-nose pliers.
~~T~~rim off excess eye pin ~~d~~ make a partial loop.
~~H~~ook partial loop ~~o~~ bottom hole.
~~F~~inish closing loop.

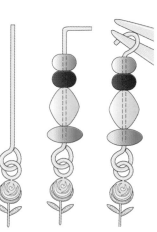

Basic Information on Artist's Materials

Artists' Materials. Heat-set Inks • Permanent Inks • Embossing Inks • Rub 'n Buff • Diamond Glaze • Spray Sealer • Paintbrush • Sponges

Dressed-Up Journals

by Jane Rouls

Personalize journals with fun shrink plastic motif. What an easy way to make gifts for special friends and loved ones. You can match all those wonderful personalities and show them how much you care!

Patchwork Heart

MATERIALS: White shrink plastic sanded on one side • 3¾" square book • Assorted rubber stamps • Black permanent ink • Watercolor cils • Pink paint pen • Black fine tip permanent marker • Sheet of pap Ultra Thin Bond adhesive • Diamond Glaze • Matte spray sealer
INSTRUCTIONS: Cut 5" heart from plastic. Using paper as a mask, sta several designs on plastic. Be creative, this is a chance to use pa images. Color with watercolor pencils, then shrink. Add dots with paint and marker. Sand edges and spray with sealer. Finish with thick coat of mond Glaze. Mount heart on book.

Basic Information for Journal Motifs

Cut out heart and mask off areas with paper.

Stamp designs on heart with heat-set ink.

Color stamped designs with watercolor pencils.

Shrink heart, sand edges and spray with sealer.

Heart Pattern

Blue Book

MATERIALS: White shrink plastic sanded on one side • 5¾" x 6½" Blue book • 3 *Stampendous* flower rubber stamps • Black heat-set ink • Watercolor pencils • Ultra Thin Bond adhesive • Matte spray sealer

INSTRUCTIONS: Cut three 3" squares and stamp images. Shrink plastic and color images with watercolor pencils. Spray with sealer and mount flowers on book.

Basic Information for Jewelry & Plastic Shrinkage

Jewelry Tools & Materials. Assorted Beads • Wire • Waxed linen thread • Jump Rings • Clasps • Needle-nose Pliers • Round-nose Pliers

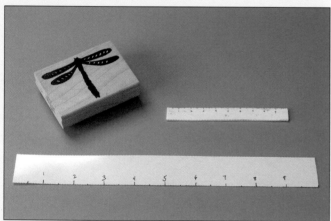

Kit Zimmerman of Lucky Squirrel has devised a wonderful way of gauging the size a piece of plastic must be in order to accommodate a complete stamp after shrinking. Cut a 2" wide strip of plastic from the same color you will be using. Mark the long side in ½" increments and shrink the strip. Measure your image or stamp with the shrunk ruler to determine the size you will have when the plastic is shrunk. Then use a regular ruler to measure and cut out your piece from the unshrunk plastic. Do this with every new batch of plastic to assure the best pieces possible.

Colorful Buttons
by Jane Roulst...

Use full size stamps with complete or partial images for this technique. By itself or in combination with the stamp first and shrink method, the results are always spectacular.

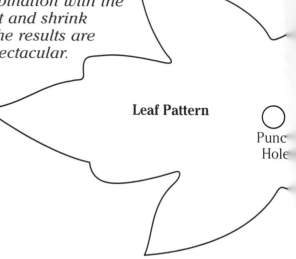

Leaf Pattern

Punc
Hole

Never have to search for a matching button again. Shrink your own for perfect results every time and in a variety of colors and patterns!

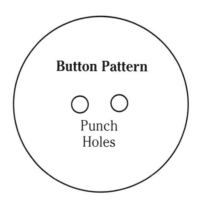

Button Pattern

Punch Holes

Multicolored Buttons

MATERIALS: White shrink pla tic sanded on one side • *Sta pendous* swirls and dots rubb stamps • Blue heat-set ink Chalk • 2¼" circle punch • ⅛ hole punch • Heat gun • Glo spray sealer

INSTRUCTIONS: Punch 2¼ circles from sanded White pla tic. Center and punch hole Rub each button with a diffe ent color chalk. Shrink ar stamp with swirls and dot Heat buttons slightly ar shape into domes over rounded surface followir instructions on page 25. Spr with gloss sealer.

*Leaves
stamped with
flower back-
grounds and
wonderful glass
beads make a
necklace filled
with natural
charm.*

Leaf Necklace

MATERIALS: White
shrink plastic sanded
on one side • *Judi-Kins*
Deco Flower back-
ground rubber stamp •
blue heat-set ink • Clear
embossing powder •
pastel chalk • Lumiere
paints (Metallic Gold,
Pearl Magenta, Pearl
Turquoise) • Assorted
sizes and colors of 6mm
& 8mm glass beads •
waxed linen cord • 6
gold charm hangers •
gold barrel clasp •
paintbrush • Heat gun •
⅛" hole punch • Nee-
dle-nose pliers • Matte
spray sealer

INSTRUCTIONS: Cut 6
leaf shapes using pat-
tern provided from
sanded White shrink
plastic and punch holes
with ⅛" hole punch.
Rub each leaf with a dif-
ferent color pastel
chalk. Shrink. Stamp
flower background with
blue heat-set ink. Dip in
embossing powder and
heat. **Do not overheat
plastic.** Remove heat as
soon as powder melts.
Paint selected areas of
design. Let dry and
spray with sealer.
Attach charm hang-
ers to leaves.
Thread charms and
glass beads on
waxed linen.

Barrel Clasp Closure

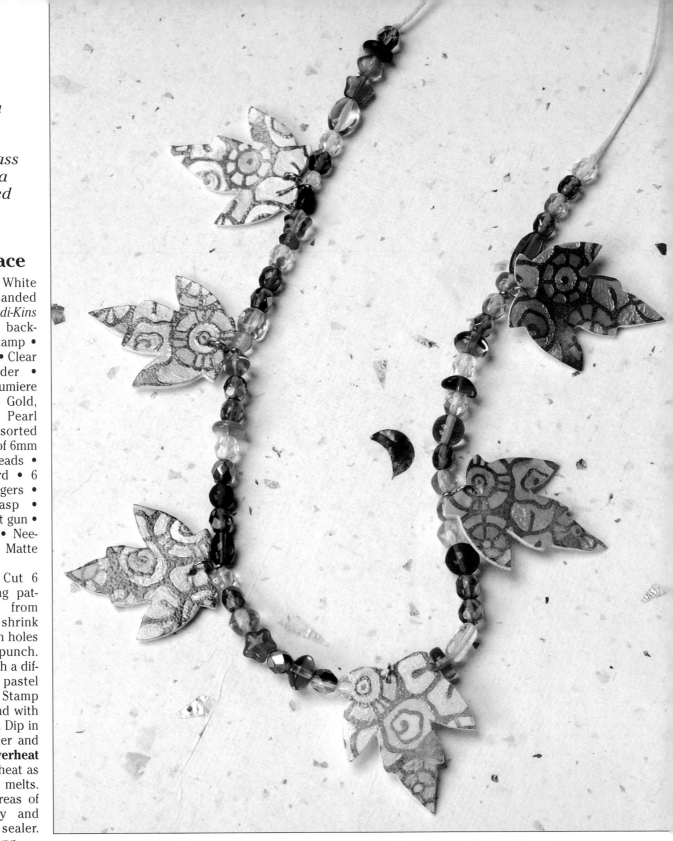

1. Cut out leaf shape and punch holes for hanging.

2. Rub leaf with chalk.

3. Shrink, stamp and paint.

How to Make Tile Motifs

Create the look of fine custom made ceramic tiles… shrink, stamp and seal with Diamond Glaze. Glued on small boxes, these tiles become statements of beautiful elegance.

1. Rub sanded plastic with colored chalk.

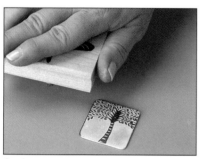

2. Shrink the sanded and colored plastic. Stamp design.

3. Sand the edges and then emboss with Black.

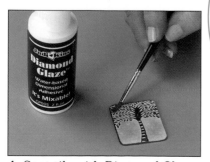

4. Coat tile with Diamond Glaze.

Beautiful Tiled Boxes
by Jane Roulst

Tree Box

MATERIALS: White shrink plastic sanded on one side • 2¼" square papier-mâché box • Tree rubber stamp • 4 wood mini candle cups for feet • Black heat-set ink • Pigment in (Black, Red, Yellow) • Clear and Black embossing powder • Yellow and Peach chalk • Diamond Glaze • Paintbrush • Heat gun • Ultra Thin Bond adhesive • Glue

INSTRUCTIONS: Cut 3½" x 3¼" piece of sanded White plastic. Rub with Yellow and the Peach chalk. Shrink. Ink tree stamp with Black heat-set ink and stamp plastic. Adjust color desired by rubbing additional chalks on image. Sand edges and emboss with Black embossing powder. Coat with Diamond Glaze and let dry overnight. Color lid and feet with Black pigment ink, dip in embossing powder and heat. Color bottom of box with Yellow pigment ink, add a little Red, dip in embossing powder and heat. Mount tile and glue feet on box.

Layered Dragonfly Box

Dragonfly Oval Patterns

MATERIALS: White shrink plastic sanded on one side • 1⅞" x 2¾" oval papier-mâché box • *Limited Edition* dragonfly rubber stamp • 4 wood 12mm balls for feet • Black and Blue heat-set ink • Black and Blue pigment ink • Clear and Gold embossing powder • Light Blue and Peach chalk • Gold paint pen • Paintbrush • Stipple brush • Heat gun • Ultra Thin Bond adhesive

INSTRUCTIONS: Cut 2 ovals from plastic using patterns. Rub large oval with Peach chalk and small oval with Light Blue making edges a little darker. Stipple edges of small oval with Blue heat-set ink. Stamp large oval with dragonfly around edges. Shrink. Shrink Blue oval and stamp dragonfly with Black heat-set ink. Sand and emboss edges of both ovals with Gold embossing powder. Glue ovals together. Color box lid with Black pigment ink, dip in Clear embossing powder and heat. Color box bottom Blue, stamp Black dragonflies, dip in embossing powder and heat. Paint feet Gold, let dry. Mount ovals and glue feet on box.

How to Finish Boxes

Rub pigment ink on the papier-mâché box. While wet, dip in Clear embossing powder, heat.

Continue to add layers of ink and powder until all surfaces are shiny.

Glue shrink plastic design in place.

4. Paint wood balls and glue for feet.

How to Make Dragonfly Ovals

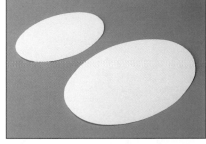

Cut ovals from plastic using patterns.

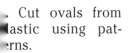

Stamp dragonflies round edge of large oval.

3. Shrink Blue oval and stamp dragonfly.

Sand edges and emboss with Gold.

5. Layer ovals and mount on box with adhesive.

Multi-Tiled Covered Box

MATERIALS: White shrink plastic sanded on one side • 2¼" square papier-mâché box • *Magenta* flower background rubber stamp • 4 wood mini candle cups for feet • Midnight Blue heat-set ink • Dark Blue and Lime Green pigment ink • Clear embossing powder • Chalk (Blue, Light Green, Red) • Diamond Glaze • Paintbrush • Heat gun • Ultra Thin Bond adhesive • Glue

INSTRUCTIONS: Cut nine 1½" squares of sanded White plastic. Rub 3 squares with each color of chalk. Shrink and stamp partial images on plastic with heat-set ink. Cover tiles with Diamond Glaze, let dry. Color lid and feet Dark Blue and box Lime Green, dip in embossing powder and heat. Mounts tiles and glue feet on box.

Leaf Triptych Motif Diagrams

Left Panel
← 2 1/8" →
4 5/8"

Center Panel
← 3 1/4" →
4 1/2"

← 3 1/2" →
Right Panel
← 3 3/8" →
4"

Faux Tiles

by Jane Roulston

Fred Mullett's delicate rubber stamp images work great with shrink plastic!

African Tile

MATERIALS: 3" and 4" squares of White shrink plastic sanded on one side • *Uptown Design* people and *Stampendous* swirl background rubber stamps • Brown and Burgundy pigment ink • Clear embossing ink • Tan embossing powder • Gloss and matte spray sealer

Thistle Tile

MATERIALS: 3½" x 4" piece of White shrink plastic sanded on one side • *Fred Mullett* thistle rubber stamp • Black pigment ink • Gold embossing powder • Green and Blue chalk • Diamond Glaze • Paintbrush

Green Flower Tile

MATERIALS: 4" square of White shrink plastic sanded on one side • *Hero Arts* flower rubber stamp • Black pigment ink • Green and Yellow chalk • Diamond Glaze • Paintbrush

Orange Flower Tile

MATERIALS: 3½" and 5" squares of White shrink plastic sanded on one side • *Hero Arts* flower and *Magenta* leaf rubber stamps • Black pigment ink • Orange and Yellow chalk • Matte spray sealer

Tile Instructions

MATERIALS: White shrink plastic sanded on one side • Assorted rubber stamps • Heat-set ink • Chalk • Corner rounder punch • Glue
INSTRUCTIONS: Cut piece of plastic. Round corners with punch. Rub with chalk. Shrink tile and stamp. Add finish.

Nature's Cards

by Jane Roulston

eaf Triptych

TERIALS: White shrink plastic sanded on one side
Rubber Stampede leaf rubber stamps • Black
t-set ink • Gold pigment ink • Clear and Gold
bossing powder • Chalk • Three 3¼" x 5¼" book
rds • Three 3¾" x 5¾" pieces of Cream hand-
de paper • 3" x 5" pieces of decorative paper
een, Blue, Copper) • Decorative paper (2" x 3¼"
ck, 2½" x 3" Light Blue, 2½" x 3¼" Brown, 1⅞" x
" Light Brown) • Four ¾" x 3" strips of Green
de paper for hinges• Gloss spray sealer • White
e

TRUCTIONS: Referring to diagrams, cut 3 pieces
stic. Rub one with Light Green and Brown chalk.
b edge of sandpaper across plastic to make
atches. Rub scratches with darker Brown. Rub
ond plastic piece with Blue and Brown. Rub third
ce with Brown. Shrink tiles. Stamp leaves with
ck heat-set ink and emboss with Clear powder.
d edges of plastic, rub with Gold ink and emboss
h Gold powder. Spray tiles with sealer.
Cover back of book boards with hand made paper,
d to front, miter corners and glue in place. Refer-
g to photo, glue decorative paper on front of book
rds. Emboss edges of smaller decorative papers
h Gold. Glue smaller papers and tiles in place.
e hinges on back ¾" from top and bottom edges
ving ½" spaces between book boards.

Faux ceramic tiles are perfect accents for elegant greeting cards that are sure to be cherished for years to come.

Rice Sheaf Card

MATERIALS: White shrink plastic sanded on one side • *Hero Arts* rice sheaf and *Magenta* texture rubber stamps • Black pigment ink • Black and Bronze embossing powder • Chalk • 4¼" x 5½" Rust folded card • Paper (2½" x 2¾" Tan, 2" x 2¼" Pale Green, 1¾" x 2⅛" Black) • Diamond Glaze • Paintbrush • Heat gun • Glue

INSTRUCTIONS: Cut 4¼" x 3¾" piece of plastic. Rub with Light Tan chalk. Stamp rice sheaf with Black ink and emboss with Black embossing powder. Adjust color by add darker chalk over embossed image with fingers. Sand edges. Coat with Diamond Glaze. Let dry overnight. Stamp Pale Green paper with texture, emboss with Bronze powder. Dot Tan paper with Black ink, emboss with Black. Referring to photo, layer and glue papers and plastic on card.

Adjusting the color with chalks after the image was stamped and embossed makes this card glow.

Fish Card

MATERIALS: White shrink plastic sanded on one side • *Fred Mullett* fish rubber stamp • Black and Green pigment ink • Black and Gold embossing powder • Chalk • 4¼" x 5½" Brown folded card • 2¼" square of Black paper • Paper strips (Rust print, Gold, Gold stripe) • Gold paint pen • Paintbrush • Heat gun • Matte spray sealer • Glue

INSTRUCTIONS: Cut 3½" square of White sanded plastic. Rub with Tan chalk. Add darker Tan and a tiny bit of Green. Shrink. Stamp Black fish and emboss with Black powder. Adjust color by adding Brown to edges. Lightly stamp pine needle texture stamp over fish using Green ink. Spray with sealer.
Emboss edges of Black paper with Gold. Cut 4 uneven strips of decorative paper. Glue strips on card, add Gold dots with pen. Glue Black paper and plastic on card.

Intaglio Jewelry

by Jane Roulston

Intaglio is the Italian term for a design produced in relief. This technique works well with all colors of plastic.

Basic Instructions

1. Heat sanded plastic until soft using a heat gun.
2. Place plastic on a smooth surface. Press stamp into sanded side of hot plastic to produce a relief image.
3. After a moment, remove stamp.

Black Hoop Earrings

MATERIALS: Black shrink plastic sanded on one side • Various texture rubber stamps • Gold metallic rub-on • Lumiere Gold paint • 12 Tan 6mm disk beads • 10 Gold charm hangers • 2 Gold ear wires • 20 gauge Gold wire • Heat gun • Round-nose pliers • Wire cutters • ¼" hole punch • Paintbrush • ⅝" dowel • Matte spray sealer

INSTRUCTIONS: Cut plastic into ten 1" to 2" long shapes. Punch holes in one end. Shrink. While hot, press texture stamp into soft plastic. Cool. Accent with Gold rub-on. Spray with sealer. Add dots with Gold paint. Spray with sealer. Make 2 hoops. Attach charm hangers to plastic pieces. Thread beads and charms on hoops as shown. Secure hoops and attach to ear wires.

Charm Hanger

Intaglio designs on Bla Translucent, Clear and Wh shrink plastic.

How to Make Wire Earring Hoop

1. Wrap 20 gauge wire aroun ⅝" dowel.

2. Make small loop at one e with round-nose pliers.

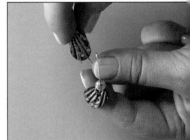

3. Thread beads and charms wire hoop.

4. Thread other end throu small loop and make anoth loop to secure.

Richly textured intaglio designs make earrings that are reminiscent of ancient Rome.

Round Black Earrings

MATERIALS: Black shrink plastic sanded on one side • *Magenta* swirl rubber stamp • Lumiere Gold paint • Gold and Green metallic rub-ons • Beads (4 Yellow 6mm flat, 6 Iridescent Black E, 4 Black 7mm disk, 2 Green 5mm disk, 2 Green leaf) • 6 Gold head pins • Pair of Gold ear wires • 2½" circle template • Paintbrush • Heat gun • ¼" hole punch • Round-nose pliers • Matte spray sealer
INSTRUCTIONS:
Cut two 2" circles from plastic. Punch holes for dangles and ear wires. Shrink and press rubber stamp in hot plastic. Rub with Gold and Green. Spray with sealer. Add dots of Gold paint and spray with sealer. Thread beads on head pins referring to photo. Make loops in tops with round-nose pliers and attach to bottom holes. Attach ear wires to top holes.

Black with Green Dangle Earrings

MATERIALS: Clear and Black shrink plastic sanded on one side • *Magenta* swirl rubber stamp • Lumiere Gold paint • Gold and Green metallic rub-ons • Green chalk • Beads (4 Green E, 6 Iridescent Bronze E, 2 striped E, 2 flat shell, 2 Green 8mm cylinder) • 6 Gold eye pins • Pair of Gold ear wires • 2¾" circle template • Paintbrush • Heat gun • ¼" hole punch • Round-nose pliers • Matte spray sealer
INSTRUCTIONS:
Cut two 2¾" circles from Black plastic. Cut six ½" x 2" Clear plastic teardrop shapes. Punch holes. Rub teardrop shapes with chalk. Shrink and press rubber stamp in hot plastic. Rub circles with Gold and Green and teardrops with Gold. Spray with sealer. Add dots of Gold paint to circles and spray with sealer. Thread beads and teardrops on eye pins referring to photo. Make loops in tops with round-nose pliers and attach to bottom holes in circles. Attach ear wires to top holes.

Attach Ear Wires to Top Holes

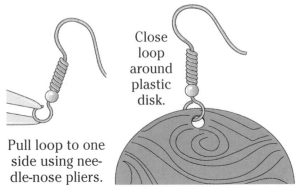

Pull loop to one side using needle-nose pliers.

Close loop around plastic disk.

Intaglio

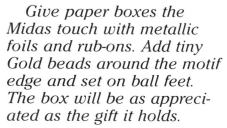

Face Box
by Sherri Burris

MATERIALS: 5" x 6" piece of Black plastic sanded on one side • *Paper Inspirations* face rubber stamp • 2½" papier-mâché square box • Gold foil • Gold leaf • ½" and ⅛" Wonder tape • Black Crystal holeless beads • 4 Gold 10mm beads for feet • Gold micro beads • Black acrylic paint • Sponge • Paintbrush • Duo glue

INSTRUCTIONS: Apply Duo glue to box bottom, let dry and apply Gold foil. Paint box lid Black, let dry. Lightly sponge duo glue on lid and apply Gold leaf. Apply ½" tape to sides of lid, add Black beads. Glue on feet. Shrink plastic, apply Gold foil and stamp face with Black ink while plastic is still hot. Using ⅛" tape, outline plastic and apply Gold micro beads. Tape plastic in center of lid.

Black & Gold Box
by Jane Roulston

MATERIALS: Black shrink plastic sanded on one side • *Judi-Kins* Primordial rubber stamp • Black pigment ink • Clear embossing powder • 2¼" square papier-mâché box • Russet Pearl-Ex • Gold metallic rub-on • 12mm wood balls for feet • Black spray paint • Heat gun • Matte spray sealer • Glue

INSTRUCTIONS: Spray box and balls Black. Rub ink on lid, dip in embossing powder and heat. Cut plastic into one 3" and four 1½" x 3¼" pieces. Shrink and press rubber stamp into hot plastic. Rub with Gold and pat Russet on some areas. Spray with sealer. Glue plastic pieces and feet on box.

How to Make a Face Box Motif

1. Shrink plastic with heat gun.

2. Stamp the foiled plastic while it is hot.

3. Apply ⅛" tape to edge and dip in beads.

Give paper boxes the Midas touch with metallic foils and rub-ons. Add tiny Gold beads around the motif edge and set on ball feet. The box will be as appreciated as the gift it holds.

Handmade Cards

by Jane Roulston

Papers and fabrics make luxurious backgrounds for stamped plastic medallions. These one-of-a-kind cards are beautiful enough to frame. Add them to your card giving collection today!

Flower Card

MATERIALS: 5" x 4½" piece of Black shrink plastic sanded on one side • Rubber stamps (*Magenta* flower, 'A La Art' dragonfly, seal) • 4¼" x 6½" Green textured card • 3⅜" x 4⅞" piece of Tan textured cardstock • Gold and Green metallic rub-ons • Scraps of Green silk • 28 gauge Gold wire • Assorted seed and bugle beads • Heat gun • Round-nose pliers • White glue

INSTRUCTIONS: Cut plastic into 3 irregular pieces. Shrink and while still hot, press flower stamp into 2 pieces and dragonfly in third piece. Cool. Rub with Gold and Green. Thread beads on wire and secure ends with small loops. Stamp seal on corner of Tan cardstock. Assemble card referring to photo.

Mad Dog Card

MATERIALS: White shrink plastic sanded on one side • *Magenta* mad dog and leaf background rubber stamps • Gold pigment ink • 4¼" x 5½" Dark Green card • Cardstock squares (2" and 3⅝" Metallic Gold, 3⅜" Dark Green, 3" Gold fleck) • Metallic rub-ons (Gold, Green, Red) • Circle templates (1⅞", 2", 3¼") • Corner rounder punch • Heat gun • Matte spray sealer • White glue

INSTRUCTIONS: Cut 3¼" circle from plastic. Heat and while still hot, press dog stamp into plastic. Cool. Rub with Gold. Buff lightly and pat on a little Green and Red. Buff. Spray with sealer.

Cut 1⅞" circle from 2" Gold cardstock and rub with Red. Round corners of remaining squares and card. Stamp front of card and Dark Green square with Gold leaves. Stack and glue squares. Cut 2" circle through center of stack. Glue plastic on Gold cardstock circle and circle in opening.

Amber Intaglio Beach Glass Necklace

MATERIALS: Clear shrink plastic sanded on both sides • Assorte[d] textured rubber stamps • Gold metallic rub-on • Chalk (Pink, Blu[e] Green, Amber) • Black waxed linen cord • Gold barrel clasp wit[h] loops • 2 charms • 13 Gold charm hangers • Assorted beads • ⅛[″] hole punch • Heat gun • Matte spray sealer

INSTRUCTIONS: Cut 11 irregular 2½" to 4" shapes, punch holes i[n] tops. Rub chalks on both sides of shapes. Shrink. While hot, pres[s] textured stamps into plastic. Rub with Gold. Spray with seale[r.] Attach charm hangers to shapes and charms. String shape[s] charms and beads on waxed linen. Attach clasp.

Combine intaglio with beach glass for unique colorful jewelry.

Green Intaglio Beach Glass Necklace

MATERIALS: Clear shrink plastic sanded on both sides • Assorted textured rubber stamps • Metallic rub-ons (Gold, Blue, Green) • Chalk (Pink, Blue, Green, Yellow) • Paint pens (Blue, Copper, Gold) • Black waxed linen cord • Gold barrel clasp with loops • 14 Gold charm hangers • Assorted colors of matte E beads • ⅛" hole punch • Heat gun • Matte spray sealer

INSTRUCTIONS: Cut 14 irregular 2½" to 4" shapes, punch holes in tops. Rub chalks on both sides of shapes. Shrink. While hot, press textured stamps into plastic. Apply rub-ons. Spray with sealer. Add small dots with paint pens and spray again. Attach charm hangers to shapes. String shapes and beads on waxed linen. Attach clasp.

1. Sand both sides of plastic

Beach Glass

by Jane Roulston

Make beautiful jewelry with the look of beach glass… sand clear plastic, rub with chalk, shrink, stamp and emboss… What could be easier?

Green Beach Glass Necklace

MATERIALS: Clear shrink plastic sanded on both sides • Green chalk • Assorted matte glass beads (Clear, Blue, Pink, Green) • White waxed linen cord • Gold barrel clasp • 1/8" hole punch

INSTRUCTIONS: Cut 9 irregular shapes. Punch holes in tops. Rub with chalk on both sides. Shrink. Attach charm hangers to shapes. String shapes and beads on waxed linen. Attach clasp.

Earrings

MATERIALS: Clear shrink plastic sanded on both sides • Assorted rubber stamps • Heat-set ink (Blue, Yellow, Amber) • Chalk (Blue, Yellow, Amber) • 10 Gold charm hangers • Assorted matte E and seed beads • 20 gauge Gold wire • 5/8" dowel • 1/8" hole punch • Heat gun • Wire cutters • Round-nose pliers • Matte spray sealer

INSTRUCTIONS: Cut 10 irregular 1" to 2½" shapes. Punch holes in tops. Rub both sides with chalk. Shrink. Stamp images with heat set inks. Let dry. Spray with sealer. Make wire hoops following instructions on page 18. Attach charm hangers to shapes. Thread shapes and beads on hoops and secure ends. Attach ear wires.

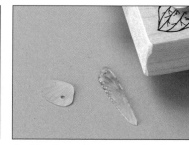

Cut out shapes and punch holes in tops.

3. Color shapes with chalk.

4. Heat and stamp designs in plastic shapes.

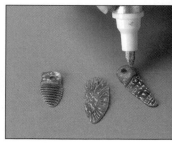

5. Add details with paint pen.

Stampscapes Box
by Steve Felt

MATERIALS: Translucent shrink plastic sanded on one side • *Stampscapes* waterfall and assorted texture rubber stamps • Black heat-set ink • Clear pigment ink • Purple stone embossing powder • 2¼" x 3" paper box • 3¼" x 3½" oval template • Assorted chalk • Gold paint pen • Heat gun • Eye shadow applicator • Glue

INSTRUCTIONS: Cut 3½" square and 3¼" x 3½" oval from plastic. Rub box lid with pigment ink, dip in embossing powder and heat. Rub chalks on plastic square and stamp with texture stamps and heat-set ink. Shrink. Stamp waterfall on oval with heat-set ink. Shrink. Color with chalks using applicator. Outline both shapes with Gold pen. Shape square and oval. Glue together. Glue on box.

Green Flower Earrings

MATERIALS: Translucent shrink plastic sanded on one side • *Magenta* flower rubber stamp • Black heat-set ink • Red and Green chalk • Beads (12 Green 4mm, 4 Blue 6mm, 2 Light Green, 2 Green and 2 Blue 8mm disk) • 2 Gold leaf charms • 4 Gold head pins • 2 Gold eye pins • Pair of Gold ear wires • ¼" hole punch • Heat gun • Round-nose pliers • Matte spray finish

INSTRUCTIONS: Cut two 2¼" plastic squares. Round corners and punch holes. Rub lightly with Green chalk and add a touch of Red. Shrink. Stamp flower and shape squares. Thread beads on head pins and eye pins. Make loops in ends. Attach charms to eye pins. Attach dangles and ear wires to squares.

Chalk Instructions

1. For bracelet, use torn paper strips to create uneven lines of color with chalk.

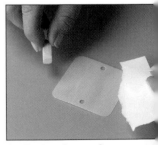

2. Fade the colors out to make soft color variations.

Yellow, Blue & Green Bracelet

MATERIALS: Translucent shrink plastic sanded on one side • Chalk (Yellow, Blue, Green) • Lumiere Gold paint • 6 Gold 8mm and 2 Gold 6mm jump rings • Hook clasp • ⅛" hole punch • Heat gun • Gloss spray sealer

INSTRUCTIONS: Cut seven plastic squares using pattern. Punch holes and round corners. Rub squares with soft Blue chalk. Tear paper into uneven strips, place on plastic and rub with Green, Blue and Yellow chalks. Fade colors out for soft variations of color. Shrink and shape. Spray with sealer. Add Gold dots. Spray with sealer. Attach squares with 8mm jump rings. Attach 6mm jump rings to end squares and add clasp to one end.

Earring & Bracelet Pattern

Punch Holes & Round Corners

Correct way to open a jump ring.

Open

Shaping

by Jane Roulston

Hot PolyShrink is very flexible and can be shaped using a dowel or a rounded piece of wood. Shaped pieces work well for jewelry, buttons, box tops and collage elements.

Basic Instructions for Shaping Shrink Plastic

Rub chalk on sanded plastic to color.

Stamp the image with heat-set ink.

3. Glue 2½" wood ball on napkin ring. Place plastic on ball.

Heat the plastic to soften. Wearing a glove, shape by placing palm of hand over plastic.

5. To make swirls, shape heated plastic around a dowel or skewer.

Spiral Necklace

MATERIALS: Clear shrink plastic sanded on both sides • Assorted texture stamps • Blue heat-set ink • Chalk (Red, Purple, Blue, Green, Yellow) • ¼" dowel • ⅛" hole punch • Gold charm hangers • Assorted glass beads • Gold barrel clasp • White waxed linen cord • Heat gun • Gloss spray sealer **INSTRUCTIONS:** Cut 17 uneven thin 1½" to 4" to pieces of plastic. Cut point on one end of each shape. Rub with chalk on both sides. Stamp various textures with heat-set ink. Shrink. While hot, shape around dowel to form spiral. Spray with sealer. Attach charm hangers to shapes. Thread shapes and glass beads on waxed linen. Attach clasp.

Faux Finishes

by Jane Roulston

This technique uses White or Translucent plastic and chalks to make beautiful faux marble, stone, bone, ivory or turquoise finishes. First apply the chalks very lightly and then add other features such as scratches and marbling textures.

Jade Box

MATERIALS: 4" Translucent and 2" White shrink plastic squares sanded on one side • 2¼" papier-mâché box • 3 *Just For Fun* Chinese character rubber stamps • Black heat-set ink • Red and Green pigment ink • Clear embossing ink • Embossing powder (Red, Gold, Clear) • Chalk (Red, Green, Light Green) • 4 wood ⅝" button plugs for feet • Diamond Glaze • Paintbrush • Heat gun • Glue

INSTRUCTIONS: Round corners of 4" square. Rub lightly with Light Green chalk. Layer with areas of darker Green and Red chalk. Stamp Chinese letter stamp lightly with Black ink. Shrink. Stamp small Chinese character with Black ink. Rub edges with Clear embossing ink, dip in Gold embossing powder and heat. Finish with Diamond Glaze.

Round corners of 2" square. Rub with Light Green and Red chalk, shrink. Stamp larger Chinese character stamp with Clear ink, emboss with Red. Emboss edges with Red.

Rub box lid and feet with Red ink, dip in Clear embossing powder and heat. Rub box bottom with Green ink, dip in Clear ink, sprinkle with Gold embossing powder and heat.

Glue squares on lid and feet on bottom of box.

Tip
For color variations, color with chalk, sand lightly and add more chalk. Have fun!

Ivory 'Antique' Buttons

MATERIALS: White or Translucent sh[rink] plastic sanded on one side • Cloud or tex[ture] stamps • Brown heat-set ink • Tan [and] Brown chalk • 1¾" circle or 2" square t[emplate] plates • ¼" hole punch • Sandpaper • H[eat] gun • Matte or gloss spray sealer

INSTRUCTIONS: Cut shape and punch h[oles] in plastic. Rub lightly with chalk. Scratch v[ith] sandpaper and rub in darker chalk. Shr[ink.] Shape following instructions on page [25.] Spray with sealer.

Turquoise Buttons

MATERIALS: White shrink plastic sanded [on] one side • '*A La Art*' cloud stamp • Brown [and] Black heat-set ink • Green and Blue cha[lk •] 1¾" circle template • ⅛" hole punch • H[eat] gun • Gloss spray sealer

INSTRUCTIONS: Cut 1¾" circles from plas[tic.] Punch holes. Lightly rub Green and B[lue] chalk into plastic. Using cloud stamp, cre[ate] veins with Black and Brown heat-set in[k.] Shrink and shape following instructions [on] page 25. Spray with sealer.

Assorted Buttons

MATERIALS: White shrink plastic sanded [on] one side • Texture rubber stamps • Assor[ted] heat-set inks • Chalk • Circle or square t[emplate] plates • ⅛" or ¼" hole punches • Heat gu[n •] Matte or gloss spray sealer

INSTRUCTIONS: Cut shapes from plas[tic.] Punch holes. Rub with chalk. Stamp textu[re] or scratch designs. Shrink and shape foll[ow]ing instructions on page 25. Spray with sea[ler.]

Faux Bone Turtle Tile
MATERIALS: White shrink plastic sanded on one side • *Rubber Stamper* turtle stamp • Black heat-set ink • Chalk (Brown, Light Brown, Ivory) • Gold paint pen • Matte spray sealer
INSTRUCTIONS: Cut 3½" square from plastic. Round corners. Very lightly rub soft Brown and Ivory chalk into plastic. With folded piece of sandpaper, make several scratches across plastic, rub with darker chalk. Shrink. Stamp turtle image with heat-set ink. Finish edges with Gold pen. Spray with sealer.

Rock Art Bracelet
MATERIALS: White shrink plastic sanded on one side • Rubber stamps ('A La Art stone texture, PSX petroglyph figures, 'A La Art cloud) • Black and Green heat-set ink • Green and Peach chalk • 8 Black jump rings • Gold lobster claw clasp • ⅛" hole punch • Heat gun • Matte spray sealer
INSTRUCTIONS: Cut seven squares of plastic using bracelet pattern on page 24. Punch holes and round corners. Rub Light Peach chalk into plastic. Add a little Dark Green chalk. Stamp cloud with Green and Black ink. Shrink. While still hot, stamp with stone texture. Stamp petroglyph figures with Black ink and let dry. Shape squares following instructions on page 25. Spray with sealer. Attach squares with jump rings. Add clasp to one end of bracelet.

Green Turquoise Earrings
MATERIALS: White shrink plastic sanded on one side • Heat-set ink (Black, Brown, Green) • Green and Peach chalk • ¼" hole punch • Beads (2 Green Turquoise nuggets, 2 Tan 10mm disk, 2 Black 8mm disk) • 2 Gold eye pins • 2 Gold ear wires • Round-nose pliers • Gloss spray sealer
INSTRUCTIONS: Cut mirror image swirls from plastic using pattern. Punch holes as shown. Rub surface and edges with chalk and stipple with inks. Shrink. Spray with sealer. Thread beads on eye pins as shown. Make loops in the ends. Attach swirls and ear wires.

Earring Pattern
Make 2
•
Reverse 1

Shrink Plastic Coloring Effects

   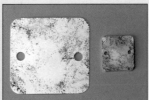 

| Translucent Plastic Green Chalk Black Heat-set Ink | White Plastic Green, Brown Chalk Sandpaper Scratches | White Plastic Green, Peach Chalk Cloud Stamped with Green, Brown, Black Ink | White Plastic Cloud Lightly Stamped with Green, Brown, Black Ink | White Plastic Orange Chalk Black Ink Veins |

Technique 8 - Gold Foil

Dragonfly Necklace Pattern

Dragonfly Necklace

MATERIALS: 2" square, 4" x 7" and 1" x 1½" pieces Black shrink plastic • *PSX* dragonfly and fleur de lis rubber stamps • Copper foil • Mayan Faerie Dust • O yard of Copper cord • 16 Metallic Gold 5mm beads Gold paint pen • Wood skewer • Glue
INSTRUCTIONS: Cut a triangle from shrink plast Shrink. While hot, roll back top of triangle to form loop. Apply Copper foil and Faerie Dust to hot plast Cut square plastic in half diagonally. Cut one piece half again. Shrink large and one small piece. While h apply foil and stamp with dragonfly on one piece a fleur de lis on other. Shrink remaining plastic piec apply foil and roll into bead. Finish edges of plast pieces with Gold pen. Thread Copper cord throu loop, tie knot close to loop. Add bead and tie knot. Gl triangles and plastic bead over cord ends. Thre remaining cord through loop, center and tie knot. Add bead, tie knot. On each side add beads and secure wi knots. Tie ends together.

Cut for Dragonfly   **Dragonfly Patterns**   Cut fo Fleur de

Cut for Bead

Gold Foil   by Sherri Burrisk

Opulent jewelry and journals are yours with the addition of gleaming gold foil. Use the positive image for cards and the negative image to decorate a journal.

1. Stamp cardstock and apply foil to stamped image.

2. Remove foil from cardstock and transfer negative image to heated plastic.

Cut necklace pieces from shrink plastic.

Heat plastic and roll over skewer form loop.

Apply foil to hot plastic.

Roll plastic around skewer to form long bead.

**Angel
Choker
Pattern**

Maiden Motif Journal

MATERIALS: 5 "x 7" and 1¾" x 7" pieces of Black shrink plastic • 5" x Black journal • Cardstock • 4" x 6" piece of Black handmade paper • *Paper Inspirations* maiden and 'journal' rubber stamps • Gold and Copper Lumiere paint • Paintbrushes • Black pigment ink • Tacky Powder • Black webbing spray • Shimmer Copper Faerie Dust • Copper foil • 28 gauge Copper wire • 10mm Amber glass bead • Glue
INSTRUCTIONS: Paint journal with Gold and Copper paint. Stipple with black ink and spray with webbing. Dust with Faerie Dust. Apply foil and Faerie Dust to handmade paper. Stamp maiden on cardstock with pigment ink. Dust with Tacky Powder and heat from below until sticky. Place Copper foil on cardstock. Lift up to produce a negative image. Shrink 5" x 7" Black plastic. While hot, transfer negative image to plastic. Shrink 1¾" x 7" plastic and apply foil. Reheat and stamp 'journal'. Glue plastic pieces on handmade paper. Thread bead on wire, coil wire to secure bead and attach to handmade paper by bending ends around edges. Glue paper on journal.

Angel Choker

MATERIALS: 4" x 7" piece of Clear plastic • *Stampers Anonymous* angel rubber stamp • Black pigment ink • Gold foil • Gold cardstock • Gold paint pen • Gold neck wire • Mayan Gold Faerie dust • Beads (5mm Gold, 9mm Red with White heart) • Yes glue
INSTRUCTIONS: Cut triangle from plastic. Stamp image with Black ink and shrink. While hot, apply Faerie Dust to image. Turn over and apply foil to selected areas while hot. Reheat if necessary. Fold top of triangle back to form loop. Glue cardstock on back, trim. Outline edges with Gold pen. Thread plastic and beads on neck wire referring to photo.

Tips

• Foils and metallic powders attach permanently to hot plastic only.
• Work quickly with foils and stamps to keep the foils true to their original color. If Copper foil is heated for too long, it will begin to tarnish.
• Heat to attach foil. Heat again to stamp intaglio style.

Flower Bracelet

MATERIALS: White shrink p[la]s[-]
tic sanded on both side[s •]
Magenta flower rubber stam[p •]
Dark Blue heat-set ink • Asso[rt-]
ed Green chalk • 8 Gold 8[mm]
jump rings • Gold spring r[ing]
clasp • Corner rounder pun[ch]
• ⅛" hole punch • Heat gu[n •]
Gloss spray sealer

INSTRUCTIONS: Cut sev[en]
squares using pattern a[nd]
round corners. Punch 2 ho[les]
referring to pattern. Rub w[ith]
chalk. Start with very Li[ght]
Green and add other shades [on]
top. Keep colors pale. Rub b[oth]
sides so backs are color[ed.]
Stamp flower on each pie[ce.]
Shrink. Sand edges. Sha[pe]
pieces following instructio[ns]
on page 25. Spray with sea[ler.]
Attach pieces with jump rin[gs.]
Add clasp.

Create this necklace
to match a favorite bea[d.]
You'll love the results!

Fish Necklace

MATERIALS: Transluce[nt]
shrink plastic sanded on b[oth]
sides • Assorted texture ru[b-]
ber stamps • Assorted he[at-]
set inks • White waxed lin[en]
cord • Beads (glass fis[h,]
Turquoise E, Peach E, [6mm]
Turquoise nugget, 12m[m]
Amber disk, 10mm Turquoi[se]
disk, 8mm Amber disk) • G[old]
head pin • 19 Gold eye pin[s •]
18 Gold 6mm jump rings • [⅛"]
hole punch • Round-nose p[li-]
ers • Gloss spray sealer

INSTRUCTIONS: Cut 18 irreg[u-]
lar shaped pieces of plast[ic.]
Rub both sides with chalk a[nd]
stamp with texture. Punc[h]
holes in tops. Shrink. Sa[nd]
edges and spray with seal[er.]
Thread beads on eye pi[ns]
referring to photo and atta[ch]
plastic pieces with jum[p]
rings. For fish dangle, thre[ad]
Turquoise E, fish, Turquoi[se]
disk and 8mm Amber bead [on]
head pin. Make loop at to[p.]
Thread 12mm Amber dis[k,]
Turquoise E and 2 Turquoi[se]
nuggets on eye pin. Attac[h to]
head pin. Thread beads a[nd]
beaded pins on linen [as]
shown. Tie knots to secu[re]
beads and tie ends together[.]

Flower Bracelet Pattern

Punch Holes

The Gallery

by Jane Roulston

The gallery includes projects that are a little more complex. Some use 2 or more techniques. All of the projects can be adapted to your personal stamp collection. Use your stamps and see what masterpieces you can create!

*To create soft, gentle
[im]ages, sand inked designs.*

[Bl]ue Moon

[MA]TERIALS: White and Clear shrink
[pla]stic sanded on one side • Rubber
[sta]mps (moon, various texture) • Blue
[hea]t-set ink • Assorted Yellow and Blue
[ch]alk • 5" x 7" piece of Gold corrugated
[pap]er • 4" x 5½" piece of Blue card-
[sto]ck • Blue and Yellow handmade
[pap]er strips • Dark Blue polymer clay •
[18] gauge Gold wire • Assorted beads
[(se]ed, E, 5mm cylinder) • Gold paint
[pe]n • ⅛" hole punch • 2" piece of ⅛"
[do]wel • Matte spray sealer

[IN]STRUCTIONS: Cut 2½" x 2" uneven
[pie]ce of White plastic. Rub with Yellow
[ch]alk. Punch holes at top and bottom.
[Sh]rink. While hot, stamp moon with
[Blu]e ink to create intaglio image. Cut
[rou]nded 2" x 1" rectangle of White
[pla]stic. Rub with Yellow and Blue
[ch]alk. Punch 2 holes. Shrink. While
[ho]t, stamp texture with Blue ink.
[Sp]ray with sealer. Rub Blue ink on
[mo]on face and buff off. Lightly sand
[pla]stic. A Light Blue tone image will
[sh]ow. Spray with sealer.
[C]ut 4 long, thin pieces from Clear
[pla]stic. Rub with Yellow and Blue
[ch]alk. Shrink. Stamp textures in
[sh]apes. Spray with sealer.
[R]ub dowel with Blue ink. Make 2
[po]lymer clay balls and press
[do]wel into clay. Bake following
[ma]nufacturer's instructions.
[Us]ing wire and beads, hang plas-
[tic] pieces from dowel.
[G]lue clay balls on Blue card-
[sto]ck. Decorate cardstock with
[pa]per strips and add Gold dots
[wi]th pen. Glue cardstock on
[Go]ld corrugated paper.

The drama of Japan is yours when you make this unique box hand colored with acrylic paint.

Japanese Box

by Steve Felt

MATERIALS: Black and White shrink plastic sanded on [o]side • 2¼" x 3¼" box • Rubber stamps (*Stamps in Mot*[ ] Japanese trio, *Embossing Arts* texture) • Black heat-set in[k] Black embossing ink • Black embossing powder • G[old] metallic rub-on • Gold paint pen • Acrylic paint (Orange, [Yel]low, Black, Pink) • Paintbrushes • Sandpaper • Spong[e •] Glue

INSTRUCTIONS: Emboss box lid with Black embossing [ink] and Black powder. Sponge Black acrylic paint on bott[om] of box.

Cut 3½" square of Black plastic. Shrink and press text[ure] stamp into plastic leaving a slight impression. Rub with G[old] and lightly sand. The Black will show through Gold leavin[g a] soft image.

Cut 2¾" square from White plastic. Cut curved sides [as] shown. Stamp lady with Black heat-set ink and shrink. C[olor] with acrylic paint. Paint edges and front border with pen[.]

Cut 1" x 2¾" rectangle from Black plastic. Shrink a[nd] stamp with bamboo texture. Glue pieces on box referring [to] photo.

**Kimono Plastic
Patterns**

Rub metallic powders on sanded Black [ ] plastic before shrinking to achieve a subtl[e] texture pattern.

Kimono Card

by Steve Felt[ ]

MATERIALS: Black shrink plastic sanded on one side • [3"] square of Clear shrink plastic • Rubber stamps (*Hero A*[rts] bamboo, *Magenta* rollagraft line texture, *Judi Kins* crane, *C*[ur]tis' *Collection* faces) • Black and Red heat-set ink • 5½[" x] 8½" Dark Green card • Papers (5" x 6" Gold swirls, 4¼[" x] 5¾" Gold, 4" x 6" Tan/White print, 3½" x 4½" Gold, 3½[" x] 4½" Red print) • Fine Gold cord • Gold metallic rub-o[n •] Diamond Glaze • Gold Pearl-Ex • Corner punch • Eye sha[d]ow applicator • Paintbrush • Glue

INSTRUCTIONS: Using pattern, cut kimono from Black pla[s]tic. Swirl Pearl-Ex powder all over plastic with applicat[or.] Stamp textures and crane with Black ink. Shrink. Stamp ba[m]boo on sleeves with Red ink. Stamp Clear plastic square w[ith] faces and Black ink. Rub Gold on bottom of kimono. Cov[er] kimono with Diamond Glaze. Glue face square as shown.

Glue kimono on Red paper and trim leaving ⅛" bord[er.] Repeat with 3½" x 4½" Gold paper and trim wider border [as] shown. Punch corners of Tan/White paper and glue c[ord] around edges. Layer and glue papers on card as shown. Gl[ue] the kimono in center of kimono papers.

**Kimono
Paper
Patterns**

Make a dainty little screen with the look of antique ivory... add a delicate butterfly handle.

panese Triptych

TERIALS: 6½" x 8" and two 3¼" x 8" pieces of White plastic
ero Arts bamboo and *Art Accents* Japanese lady rubber
mps • Black heat-set ink • Chalk (Yellows, Green, Browns) •
le butterfly • 14 Gold 8mm jump rings • Two 3½" pieces of
mboo skewer • ¼" hole punch • Gloss spray sealer • Sand-
er • Glue

TRUCTIONS: Cut plastic pieces going the same directions on
stic. Sand small pieces on both sides and large piece on one
e. Punch 7 holes at 1" intervals ¼" in from both long sides of
ge piece. Align side pieces and punch holes to match large
ce. Rub both sides of small pieces and one side of larger
ce with soft Yellows, Browns and Green chalk. Scratch with
dpaper and rub with darker Brown chalk. Shrink. A toaster
n is recommended.

tamp bamboo on inside of small pieces and Japanese lady
large piece with Black ink. Spray both sides of plastic pieces
h sealer. Hinge with jump rings. Rub skewers with Black ink
l insert in hinges. Glue butterfly on one side for door handle.

Doll Patterns

Tiny folk dance a jig on necklaces and earrings. These pieces are sure to be conversation starters.

Three Dolls

by Stephanie Jones Rubiano

GENERAL MATERIALS: White shrink plastic sanded on one side • Rubber stamps • Black heat-set ink • Chalk • 24 gauge Gold wire • 6mm to 8mm Gold jump rings • Round-nose pliers • Needle-nose pliers • 1/8" hole punch • Gloss spray sealer

GENERAL INSTRUCTIONS: Draw doll parts on White plastic. Cut out. Punch holes in head, body, arms and legs. For wire hair, punch 4 or 5 holes at top of head. Clean off any smudges with a paper towel. Lightly rub chalk on plastic if desired. Stamp designs on doll parts with heat-set ink. Shrink. If desired, color edges with paint pen. Spray with sealer.

Make small spiral in end of 2" piece of wire with pliers. Place arm behind body and line up holes. Push wire through holes. Turn body over and pull wire taut. Make another loop to create a joint and allow arm movement. Cut off excess wire. Place body and arm between needle-nose pliers and gently squeeze to tighten wire joint. Repeat for other arm and legs. Cut 1" pieces of wire and twist through holes on top of head and make spirals for hair. Attach head to body with 6mm jump ring.

Mermaid Necklace - *Fred Mullett* fish and *Moon Rose* face rubber stamps • Green chalk • Two 5mm Brass shell charms • Green 24 gauge wire • 24" of 2mm Black cord • Green 9mm bead • Gold paint pen • Glue • Red acrylic paint

INSTRUCTIONS: Make tail using fish stamp, Black ink and Green chalk. Stamp face. Shrink. Add dots and color edges of

legs with pen. Paint lips Red. Assemble as shown. Add an 8mm jump ring to top of head. Thread cord through jump ring and glue ends in bead.

Queen Necklace - Rubber stamps (*Stampers Anonymous* words, *Teesha Moore* letters, *Moon Rose* face) • 8mm and 12mm Brass crown charms • 24 gauge Red wire • 24" of 2mm Black cord • Red 9mm bead • Gold paint pen • Glue • Red acrylic paint

INSTRUCTIONS: Stamp face. Stamp words on arms and legs and letters on body. Shrink. Color edges of body with pen. Paint lips Red. Assemble as shown. Glue crown to top of head. Add 8mm jump ring to crown on head. Thread cord through jump ring and glue ends in bead.

Earrings - *Stampers Anonymous* clockworks rubber stamp • Tan chalk • Two 14mm watch faces • Pair of Gold ear wires • 4 watch gears • Gold and Silver paint pens • 1/16" hole punch • Glue

INSTRUCTIONS: Rub body pieces with chalk and stamp. Shrink. Color edges of body, arms and legs with Silver pen. Color edges of arms and legs Gold. Punch holes at top and bottom of watch faces. Assemble as shown. Attach ear wires.

Shrink Art Designers

Jane Roulston is a stamp artist who lives in Amarillo, Texas with her husband, 2 children, 3 cats, one dog, one hamster and one prairie dog. Jane earned her Bachelor of Fine Arts degree at the University of Houston in printmaking.

Jane has taught classes all over the country. Her work has been published and she designs for Papers by Catherine. Plastic changed her life. She loves teaching and thanks all the store owners who have given her a chance 'from the bottom of her heart'.

Stephanie Jones Rubiano is a studio artist who has taught stamping, paper crafting and polymer clay classes. Her work has graced the pages of several magazines and sells in stores and galleries all around the United States.

Sherri Burrisk is a stamp artist who lives and works in Conroe, Texas. She has been a representative for several stamp companies and has taught rubber stamping classes.

Sue Bell, a stamp artist f Amarillo, Texas is active on internet and has stamping frie all over the world. She has b published in Vamp Stamp N and Stamping Arts & Crafts. has a master's degree in elen tary education. She taught scl for 15 years and on retirem began teaching adults the won ful world of rubber stamping.

Steve Felton is a stamp a working in Amarillo, Texas. H very inventive and loves to what stuff will do'.